The News as Usual

MARY BURRITT CHRISTIANSEN POETRY SERIES
Hilda Raz, Series Editor

Mary Burritt
Christiansen
Poetry Series

The Mary Burritt Christiansen Poetry Series publishes two to
four books a year that engage and give voice to the realities of
living, working, and experiencing the West and the Border as
places and as metaphors. The purpose of the series is to expand
access to, and the audience for, quality poetry, both single
volumes and anthologies, that can be used for general reading as
well as in classrooms.

Also available in the Mary Burritt Christiansen Poetry Series:

After Party: Poems by Noah Blaustein
Gather the Night: Poems by Katherine DiBella Seluja
The Handyman's Guide to End Times: Poems by Juan J. Morales
Rain Scald: Poems by Tacey M. Atsitty
A Song of Dismantling: Poems by Fernando Pérez
Critical Assembly: Poems of the Manhattan Project by John Canaday
Ground, Wind, This Body: Poems by Tina Carlson
MEAN/TIME: Poems by Grace Bauer
América invertida: An Anthology of Emerging Uruguayan Poets
    edited by Jesse Lee Kercheval
Untrussed: Poems by Christine Stewart-Nuñez

For additional titles in the Mary Burritt Christiansen Poetry Series,
please visit unmpress.com.

THE NEWS AS USUAL

Poems

Jon Kelly Yenser

University of New Mexico Press | Albuquerque

Library of Congress Cataloging-in-Publication Data
Names: Yenser, Jon Kelly, 1945– author.
Title: The news as usual : poems / Jon Kelly Yenser.
Description: Albuquerque : University of New Mexico Press, 2019. |
    Series: The Mary Burritt Christiansen Poetry Series |
Identifiers: LCCN 2018024530 (print) | LCCN 2018025972 (e-book) |
    ISBN 9780826360212 (e-book) | ISBN 9780826360205 (pbk. : alk. paper)
Classification: LCC PS3625.E48 (e-book) | LCC PS3625.E48 A6 2019 (print) |
    DDC 811/.6—dc23
LC record available at https://lccn.loc.gov/2018024530

Cover photographs courtesy of Jean Wimmerlin on Unsplash (top) and
    Shutterstock (bottom).
Cover designed by April Leidig
Composed in Dante MT Std 11.5/13.5

For Pamela and our family, Jessup and Becca

Contents

Part III

Part IV

Part I

Invocation to Lucretius

O Lucretius, my devious
mapper of happenstance
and master of mixing
fluke with gravity,
kindly show us the way,

zigzag into this mess
that we might see
consequence for what it is,
that we might not lose
ourselves in confusion.

Railing against People Railing against Kansas

First of all the fields
are not endless and there's no point
saying that just for emphasis.
This is a soccer field.
That is a field of alfalfa.
You can see the difference.
That's kefir corn,
and those are beans, and that's
something else, and so on.
The Rockies will rise by and by.

Second, there's an order
here you can't imagine.
You have to imagine the old days
when not much
was measured (mirage
or monotony) until you got
to the next mission.

Third, no one mushes
from Nome to Fairbanks in February,
but you drove from Joplin
to Junction City in August.

Stay home or fly across
or make a phone call,
but stay out of the fields
of canola brighter than neon,
the burnt umber of milo.

The State Bird

The meadowlark's song,
a knot of wonder,
unparsed as kanji,
opens in white space
and closes there, shaping

both—a maze
of immeasure, a wild
scoring, a warbling
puzzle we can't solve
easily, if ever.

But say we could.
Would we straighten it,
make a line going
somewhere, a route,
one point and the next,

a map of the in
and out of the fields
we surveyed in the old days,
plotting even then
the endnote here?

Lunch at the Flint Hills Diner

I don't think there's a dangerous line
to cross anywhere in this county.
It's all squared up and agreed to.
We don't live on the edge of anything:
no canyons, no shores. A little gravity.

Not even the old folks can recall
when the cottonwoods were cleared
for plowing. Now there's no end
of land. All day the regulars come
and go and we speak—greetings, family,
the weather, the football team this fall.

But this girl, summer help, this morning
rolled up her sleeves to show us
ridges of flesh on her arms, healed
now but as carefully measured once
as yard lines on the high school field.

The Salesman

1. *Reviews His Territory in a Meeting*
My map's always in my head,
the roads, thin as veins in an eyelid,
trickle through the gashed prairie
east of here—heaps of slag, sickly scrub,
rusty milo. It's no territory for faint hearts.
Last week I clocked a six-point buck
near Coffeyville and still made my quota.
At this morning's meeting, there's Sheila
across the way in her flowery blouse,
an intersection of rosy silk and freckled crevice.
I'm put in mind of a map of flatland relief,
that fine triangle of towns you can trace
driving north from the mines: Coyville
to Thrall to Climax. Look it up.

2. *Talks Like Everybody Else*
I talk for a living, and usually it's fun.
It gives me something to do,
and as a rule it does no harm.
There's a place for everything.
I fit in stories as I can.
In this way people think you're like them—
same as talking about their weather
or the way you came. Always,
always tell a joke. I hear the same ones,
but I try to hand out fresh ones.
I keep a catalog in mind, sorted by location
(a bar, a golf course, the gates of heaven)
and situation (you're drunk or driving or dead,
you're talking to a dwarf or your wife or god).

3. *Reviews His Territory in the Car*

Take one hard look. They don't call
this country the Little Balkans
for nothing. Think about it: the neighbors—
Okies and Show-Me's—don't claim it.
People here got no use for each other
or this land, done for, flat-out
ugly as coyotes—slag and tailings,
stunted oak, the steam of contagion.
On the road I roll up the windows
no matter the season. I don't breathe in.
There's good fishing, I'm told,
for small-mouth bass in the pools of cold
cold water that seeps in the gashes. Catch
what you will. I'd rather eat mud cat.

4. *Gets Fired*

It's hard to say what happened
exactly in order. We don't have agendas
on Mondays, just the usual muzz and doughnuts
and Sheila confusing as usual.
But several colleagues said later
that several colleagues had said
they'd had higher hopes for my quota.
I do know this: the boss wore mauve,
her blouse unbuttoned two from the top.
And I know she had darkness
between her breasts and creases like knives
in her sleeves. Her smile filled her mouth.
She said, "What's expected is understood."
I saw her teeth, and they weren't good.

5. *Reviews His Career in a Bar*

You know what? Guess what?
I was looking for a job when I got
that one. It's a proven fact that people
will buy things, need them or not.
I am not worried. In the beginning
was the word and that word was
Sales. Hallelujah! What a deal!
I can sell you chipped ice for your igloo.
I don't need this noise. Shove this route
where the light don't shine, O my buckaroos,
and turn me loose! I'm free,
free at least until the first,
and by then, by God, somebody
will need something I can move.

Fishing on the Ninnescah

Once on the sluggish Ninnescah
the boy's line got snagged
on a cottonwood and so
he whipped the rod
back and forth and the sun
caught the fiberglass
in rainbow parabolas
until the hook sang loose
and followed the line
back to the web of flesh
between his thumb and finger.

At the scream
the father saw first
the eye of the bluegill
he was cleaning on a rock
and thought, "Oh, my God,"
and went running with the tackle box.

With the pliers
he snipped the shank
and pushed until the hook
appeared in the boy's palm.
He pulled it through
and the wound bloomed
red around a muscle
as white as a grubworm.

Meanwhile the bluegill
seemed to be sunning on the rock
but was losing its sheen
like a river rock dulls

out of water, was turning
the color of its bones.

By the time the father
got back to his work
it was hard as the rock,
its eyes bright as mica.

Current Events

1.

In the early morning an inside thing
moves of its own accord: a cereal box
rattles in the cupboard, a slack
floorboard gives back my steps two steps later.
Things move unexhausted yet
in early April in the Midwest.

One hopes. History may not exactly
snicker at the latest catastrophe,
but it has a place for it. Things
have always been getting worse, I think,
and just now the paper boy peddles by
and the dogs bark in half surprise.

2.

The meanest word on the block
belongs to the jay, head cocked
in the willow, eyeing night crawlers
glued all winter in sex. Drizzle
brings them up through clods
and sodden leaves full of promise.
If the jay should come out
in any event and strike our hearts
with light and a blue almost luminous
and a black like the night
behind neon, would we be lifted
with his furious diligence?

3.

He never has a casual glance,
his blood burning too fast
for distraction. There's a slug's trail,
a painterly blur as crooked and silver
as Christmas tinsel strung below the privet
we planted last fall. We see this
will be the year for the hedge
to square those frenzied raspberries
on the north slope. It's all begun
to stir, the urge, the swollen
shoots. As usual the jay's eager
and beady with detail.

4.

All winter all white the snow drifted
south, stitched with the topsoil
of farmers who thought they'd plow early
and get a jump on the green future.
But a late wind put it all in the bank!
There's a price to pay in the fall.

All winter I doodled in the long dark.
The frost on the pane inclined to foothills.
Marginalia fell off. Novels I read accomplished fact
but rarely character and never cause
and effect. Meanwhile my friends mailed me
volumes, dense opacities perfectly bound.

5.

By now the light's balancing
inside and out on the sill's edge
and on the edge of the butcher block
too courteous for words. Unfold the news:
a plane crash in southern France
has killed 103. Every other name
(in dizzy agate on 9-A) seems familiar.

Elsewhere someone's reached accord
in a foreign affair as though it were high fruit.
Finally from Florida the warmth of box scores,
the elegance of plot by number.
                    Outside the jay's refrain:
give and take and take again.

6.

I'd fill the air with that cry—
not the profligate starling's squawk
and not the flicker's wing shying away
in the maple's shade. No, the jay.
The jay raises his head like a hatchet
and chases the flicker higher.

No, it should be quieter than that.
Day breaks and half-awake my son
begins to hum against my chest.
It is my own voice. This fits
his latest notion: that I will grow younger
as he becomes a man. Parallel, opposite.

7.

Played false by dawn the jay's
most luminous on bluest days,
a matter of refraction,
blue because the sky is.
              Yesterday
we found a tail feather
layered in yellow and gray
and striped black as the ace of spades.
If pure color suffers no influence,
as Newton said, and depends not on the length
of study, but of wave, then
the heart of the wild carrot cannot
be bruised. We cannot assume
this bird holds a candle to the art
of human and intimate abuse.

8.

The flicker comes and goes cadging
light, a candid wing. The first thing
yesterday we took a walk: a night crawler
in the privet, a purplish vein,
and the slug, the fool's amethyst,
surely feed the jay. Whatever he owns,
he eats. It's a simple lesson.
Sometime before dawn I listen
to my son breathing, holding my own breath.
And then we breathe together.
Things change, he's noticed, but nothing's
gone in the process, he thinks. First thing
this morning we take a walk,
looking for examples of his logos,
opposed as we are to loss.

The Disambiguation of Katydids

When I was a kid
we didn't bother
locust from katydid
hopper from not.

When I was a kid
in the neighborhood
we did what we did.
We did what we could.

Katydids don't
have the horns hoppers do.
What we called "locust"
was the cicada instead,

which left its case
in the rings of tar
on the trees of shade
all summer all the days

when I breezed
down Coolidge Street
where the elms were leafy
and never diseased.

When I was a kid
in the neighborhood
we didn't do much.
We didn't do good.

Most of this is so
I suppose. The katydid
waves its feelers, I know,
in the wind in which

the grasshopper spits.
We unstuck cicada shells
and stuffed the slippery bits
down the throat

of Charley next door.
There was no reason
I know of, nothing more
than what we did. When

I was a kid we did
what we did and we did
what we could
and we never did better.

Revisiting the Weather

For Becca

I'd forgotten that
the front edge of a front
seems its opposite,

a long in-drawing,
a sough up high in the elms,
in the maples a sigh.

Just before the first drops
icy and big as dimes change
things for the better

the wind comes up.
You never mistake the storm
for what came before.

I grew up agape
and breathless in this weather
and the pulse it kept.

Broadcast

Whatever did Dirk do
with that name before
he shaped a widow's peak
and donned a cardigan
for credibility's sake?
In childhood, I mean,
before he became
the anchor man
on KAKE
in the happy time
of test patterns,
a plains Indian
in a war bonnet, a time
when all the kids
on the block
were almost like him,
when they called out
when he was it
at kick-the-can,
all those wavy evenings
humming with bugs?
Olly, olly ocks in free,
Dirk. Ready or not.

Shagging Flies

He stands in the shade of an elm, his hat tipped back, his hand on his hip, a bat on his shoulder. He is on balance casually, waiting for the peg. If it's off line or if it takes a bad hop, bouncing off the schoolhouse wall, he cups his hands and calls, "Good arm" or, "Way to hum." And lopes after it. He will make you wait. He is, after all, in the shade of the elms.

The bat still tilted on one shoulder, he bends to the ball and tosses it up in one motion. And now in double time he straightens and cocks the bat and brings it through. He lays into it. You lose the ball off the bat in the tan brick of the schoolhouse. And then in the trees. You must read the swing when it comes off the bat, or it's too late. By the time you hear the echo, the ball has come clear of the elms and through a trick of the eye has become a black point in the cloudless blue of the afternoon. It is August in Kansas. If you haven't begun to move, you won't catch up, because he hits it on the nose. He never loops the swing. You will have the paradoxical thought that although the ball will hang there forever, you have to run now. Your cleats chunk on gravel. You try to run on your toes because your dad told you that if your heels hit, the ball will jump in midair. He said that DiMaggio had a nine-foot running stride. That is why he is called "The Clipper." You track the fly ball. You try to glide on the gravel.

The rhythm seems incontrovertible: the crack of the fungo, the chunk of the cleats, the ball high and dark as a bird, the thin clap if you make the catch in the pocket the way you're supposed to, the arc of the peg. He stands in the shade. You have been doing this forever, but soon enough you will trade places. Louis will leave the elms and come into the sunshine and shag flies.

Making Peace

In Memory of Louis Royston

I'd like to hear a story for once
in which the boy who shoots a rabbit
in a corn row feels good afterward,
cradling the British Enfield
he's ordered through the mail
and couldn't wait to use.

Or this: a working mom
on her way to meet a boyfriend
at Doc's Steakhouse smashes
a spider on the baseboard
of her kitchen and leaves it there
to blend in.

Or, here are two boys
in Wichita in July setting fire
to an anthill in a crack of asphalt,
using model airplane glue
as accelerant. Later they go in
to watch *Spin and Marty*.

That was a long time
before Louis went off to war.
I never wrote to his mother,
not because I never thought
about him or July or fire.
Maybe I thought
I'd like to hear another story

that ends another way for once
even if it's no more true
than the first one. There are two boys
plinking at rabbits,
burning in the heat.

When I Got Back

There was a story
I was going to tell you
taking place in Kansas
in a neighborhood
you would have liked
where I got lost
after nearly going to sleep
on the turnpike as usual
taking an exit for a town
I didn't know
on a river we've heard of.
I drove over the bridge
the water as brown
as I remembered
and then turned left
onto a street in full leaf
in deep shade
in oak and maple and elm
whose trunks were ringed
with tar against cicadas
that were not singing
then in early afternoon
but their song was waiting
in the trees for evening I thought
because no one comes back
I'm going to tell you now.

Lucretius Applied on the Plains

Imagine a drizzle
so perfectly windless
(how rare out here!)
it serves to illustrate
the idea of gravity
in a children's book
the path of each drop
so finely drawn
it might be broken—
but no matter
since there is no wind.
On the next page
something goes kerflooey
when one drop swerves
without cause into another
and that into the next
and so on and so that
now we can never count
on tomorrow.

Part II

Spring Fever Blues

O huddle and glum
of spring O blossoms
opening OK
but only slowly
in this cold Ting Ting

a framing hammer
ringing on sinkers
nearby like water
cold cold on your wrist

Hopeful isn't it
all this industry?

now rat rat-a-tat

someone's truss today
will be raised Huzzah!

Let's call it good for
now no end in sight.

The Abundant Shame of Spring, the Forsythia

explodes one morning, and the holly sharpens
its hooks the next. The hawks have come back
to the lodgepole. This day begins with close heat
and wetness nearly herbal, thick with transition.
The quince spills across the fence with Walter's yard.
Our dog roots for what fell from the fledgling last year,
once-promising scents become artifact, floor plan.
Here's some shred—old, intricate weave, fabric
or flesh—and here a wheat stalk from elsewhere.
Imagine! Close your eyes. Floaters like amoebae
divide on your rosy lids. Vacant parens.
Imagine this stalk, ornate as art deco,
as organized, offering us gilt antennae
and the famished thousand mouths of insects.

Early Work

Not yet unstrung
another dawn
tuning up:
a drum thump
a round horn note
sleet on a tin roof
like something shaken
from the blue sky
of Kandinsky: whimsy
a sprung spring.
That I can do all this
and the dog unstirred!

And now the radio:
a short-waisted
unbreasted
small-wristed
girl in a Resistol
a nice name like Lilly
or Lucinda singing
a blues you can live with.
Still strung
alive with crepitus
I'm out of bed again
and the screw turns
and turns.

At 4:48

Our brown Lab circles three times
to the left and settles on the rug.
He swallows once, twice, and sighs.
He does it all again. My doctor
the chemist said dogs suffer
from OCD, their serotonin retrieved
too often.
　　　Ours shifts and swallows
and so on again. But "suffer?" What jowl
wrinkle is wrong, what gob of slobber
out of place?
　　　I roll over to read the clock.
Someone's running outside, splat
splat in the drizzle every morning,
or the pinkish dawns of spring
every day just like that.

We Lose Two Dogs

Our dogs are dying. First Walter's Emma
toppled in the blown forsythia, full
of holes inside, he told me after the necropsy.
In June our black Lab began leaving herself
every evening, flushing quail, fetching
birds faster than ever in her cedar bed.
She went down one day and could not rise
from her own mess. That left us one apiece.
And not for long, I said, not long enough.
"It's the same old, same old," Walter said.
"Every so often it's the end of everything."
The hard-headed quince was beginning.
Just then we were standing in our yards,
the chain link between us and nothing else.

There's a Dog Loose

There's a dog loose in the neighborhood
and a man chasing. "Bear!" he yells,
turning my corner on Fifth, "Bear!"
but the dog trots away, the way
they do when they hear you. The man
collapses to a knee: "Fuck a duck,"
his hands taking his weight forward
like a sprinter in the blocks, head down,
but at his end, exhausted. He looks up
at me looking at him from the garden
where I'm messing with raspberries,
and then we both watch the dog, a terrier
with a ridiculous rump and stubby legs,
try for a straight path in the middle
of the street.
        "Come on," I say, "we'll take
my truck." He gets in without a word
and then I smell him—not unfamiliar
suddenly for a Sunday: body and whiskey
and even the bright outdoors. Like my father
he looks steadily ahead when I look at him.
When the dog turns left on Blaine and I note
this route, the man says, "I know . . . I know
where he's going."
        But *I don't*, and before
I can say that and add, "Then why are we doing this?"
we're at the corner and he's out of the truck
on a crooked run like a coyote, quartering
the courtyard of the Elysian Fields Apartments
where the dog circles and squats.

The Elysian Fields Apartments

At block's end, at neighborhood's edge,
a block-long set of apartments, the Elysian Fields,
sometimes called by the kids who live there
White Harlem, as if they knew—an elongated U
of two-story units on slabs, sided with clapboard.
It was a barracks for the air cadets of '42.

Today a bike, two hibachis, a perambulator
border the courtyard that was the parade ground.
Almost any summer afternoon you can stand there
and hear rambunctious sex on the second floor,
someone soldiering on in the heat.
                          There's a kid
who lives there who comes by our yard
to play with our dog, tossing whatever's brought
until they're both done in. And so one day
in July, the dog heaving and slobbering,
I stepped out. "He's a little tired," I said.
"You probably ought to give him a rest."
And the boy, seven or eight, nodded, a slimy ball
at arm's length. I thought to offer him
something more. "His name is Fred,"
and the boy, not defiant and not afraid,
"I call him Brownie." I went inside
on that last good word.
                          That dog will fetch
as long as you toss—leap for Frisbees, field balls
off the fence, deliver a stick not even scratched.
He has a soft mouth, as they say, bred to carry
things without damage, and he is brown.

Great Horned Owl

Come out, little ones, it's time for school,
he calls over Walter's yard, wheeling
for the hungriest ones. One simple rule:

early to rise, easier to fool,
coos the voice of wisdom, billing.
Come out, little ones, it's time for school.

Who's game? Ah hoo, hoo, who'll
own up to thrall, easy thrilling
for the hungry ones. One simple rule:

I mean truly to please you, my jewel.
Who else knows how? Who else will sing,
Come out, little ones, it's time for school.

The great horned owl counts coup
on skunk and porcupine on a moth's wing!
For the hungriest one, one simple rule.

Ah hoo and who's queued up so soon
(too soon! we cry at once) once the bells ring?
Come out, little ones, it's time for school.
For the hungriest ones, one simple rule.

Walter Fails

A week ago Walter fell and broke
his biggest bone. He was tying a shoe
when he crashed against the tub.
                    If the knee
had been his own, something else—a muscle
or ligament—might have come loose.
As it was, his new titanium joint
was screwed tight and good as guaranteed
for life, and so the femur snapped instead.

It must have hurt like hell.
I missed the hullabaloo—the ambulance,
the EMTs wheeling him away.

He's back home now, pinned again,
but I haven't seen him. The downstairs parlor's
become a sick bay, I guess, because I hear
through the window Walter and his therapist
working every morning: a ratcheting whirr,
some whimpers, soft thumps like pillows
plumped. I imagine a wired contraption
and Walter walking upside down in this dark
version of the *Cirque du Soleil*.
                    We sent pizza
over last night and this morning found a note
of thanks under our door, the text in a clean hand
over his crawling signature. We watch
for his reappearance on his deck
for cocktails, but nothing yet.

Walter and I Play Clue

Things change. For instance:
this wall-to-wall carpet
used to be bright parquet.
My favorite token, the lead pipe,
has become flimsy aluminum.

And Scarlet in our day
was a Hollywood siren,
a version of Lizabeth Scott—
classic noir with her blonde forelock
and one eye peering out.

Now she's Asian, confusing.
I can't imagine her doing it
with anything as colonial
as a revolver. But secret passages
still connect the corners,

and Plum is still useless,
bundled in his seedy tweeds,
driving down for the shooting.
Over sherry he continues grousing
to the Colonel about tenure.

I accuse Plum on principle,
a whiner. But Walter flashes a grin
and the truth: he's got him.
And he's got me, I suppose.
I could have expressed

mere suspicion, but at our age
I'd rather know something
before the next roll. I'd like to know
the victim's name at least,
and all the false steps

that led to this mess. The guests—
his so-called friends—must know
most of the story. They traipse his halls,
chalk his cues, play the piano
that's badly out of tune.

They must gossip about him
in his absence. But no one lifts
a finger to help with prints or prove alibis,
the blue-collar work that's left for us.
Meanwhile their linens

collect in closets upstairs.
Mrs. White bones the chickens
and fetches Chablis. There's
a polished surface to their game,
but things can worsen.

They led swirling lives once,
but so many years have straightened
their affairs, and now they retire separately,
with copies of *Colliers* and *Life*,
hoarding clues for the last crime.

Another Owl in the Neighborhood

Something's wrong
waking us in the dark
an owl's counter song

in velveteen a new voice
on the block, younger
and not so cunning

as the other spooning
out hunger. Out of bed
I step over the dark sprawl

of our last dog.
Last week he fell down
the stairs, got up lopsided.

He's lost direction—
that's the way it goes,
the way it's always gone

so that now the song
of the owl is still
a siren's song, but not

yet sung by a siren
the way it goes—
the way it's always gone.

Fall Leaves Blues

What's done is done
almost now almost
all the dun leaves
have come undone

come spinning down
in tiny clatters
on frozen ground
in the cold cold wind

the wind unloosed
thus undoes us
all almost none
ever our doing

what's done was done
long time coming down.

Cleaning Up in October

You know spring's usual
promise of shoot and bloom,
aroma of fresh riot

gives way to summer,
all hot air and appetite.
Our backyard hawks

mated, scraping
the sky like blue tin every dawn
until we wanted to scream.

Everything grew
until it was cut: even the wheat
in the fields slumped like loaves.

But now fall's first snap has
brought us back to earth and leaves
and the light leaving early.

High noon. Our block thrums
with industry: rakes and brooms,
spades, black plastic.

Walter's yard next door
and next the new couple's new walk
have squared our corner.

The guy with the Harley
sits on his porch with a radio,
his machine detuned.

For our part we start
in the backyard's back corner,
under the lodgepole

where the hawks nested.
Each pitchfork full turns up
something for the dog,

twitching, delirious
in a thick rhythm of root
and drool. Under our heels

gristle and pine needles grind
powders in our eyes.
Scintillant fall!

Another layer: slabs
of leaves, sodden lumps, hawthorns,
and then suddenly

the girlish skeleton
of a squirrel nearly picked
clean to a soft shine.

The dog backs away
knowing nothing's here to know.
We leave it, intricate,

nearly assembled,
and rake the rest together.
But that night in bed

I imagine Walter's cat
unbelled in our backyard
and the great owl

quiet as a moth
over the soccer fields, listening
for the click

of the smallest teeth
all over town, from love, habit,
and the coming cold.

An Elegy ahead of Time

O bony-ass Fred,
O Freddy, you bag of bones.
It used to be your haunches
rippled fairly in the field.

Now look at you. And smell:
your breath's uneven
and foul as swamp water.
I smell across the room

something decaying deeper,
creeping through the roots of your teeth,
blackened as they are
like burnt stumps in timber.

Getting to your feet, back end
last, wobbling at the window
and backlit, you shake stuff loose,
an instant nimbus!

Jowl gobbet and ooze,
mucus and eye slime, one eye
a glassy fog and useless
except sideways. I love you.

O Fred of bones, sway
back and sag, Fred of the gnarled sockets.
It used to be your freestyle
twists at Frisbee were tens across.

And now I shoo you out
and down the steps of ice
slick as cellophane. You take them
headlong in obedience,

a foolish, fearless act,
and now you stand at the bottom,
panting, upright, refusing failure,
to take the air. This can't last.

O Fred of slime and slick,
of glorious effluvia,
I will miss you. You and I
wasted our best hours in company.

Early Snow

"Well," Walter says, "the good news
is you'll see me coming in the dark—
great balls of fire!"

Here we are, knee-deep
in snow a week before Christmas,
shovels in hand, caps and mittens,

working toward each other
on the front walk. I laugh too long
and say I've heard it's good

to keep your spirits up.
"Yes, yes, I have a good sense
of humus." It's a moment

before I hear the dark in that.
I'm one scoop's width
toward the two sticks of lath

Walter has planted either side
of the drive so he can park.
The near one must be my lawn.

I shovel to it and stop, but Walter,
who has more method, will not
be hurried—one scoop left, one right,

and pause. And again.
At last at the far stick:
"That's enough." He nods

at the clotted ruts in the drive,
oil and ice like porphyry.
"Rock salt, here. Give it time."

Part III

Transition

We left that winter
before we lost Walter
or vice versa. We left
the alley of raptors

and rattling edges,
of stumps and rumors.
We left behind the guy
with his Harley rap-

rapping catty-corner.
We left our neighbor's
excessive tulips, asleep
but waiting for the alarm

of spring like kudzu—
too much yellow before
coffee, more yellow
than yolks. Good-bye.

The hawks anyway
were gone once the guy
across the alley cut down
the lodgepole. The sun

flooded our garden
and the Romas went wild
in the soil made rich
with fledgling gleet.

The cilantro flourished,
but it wasn't enough
for us when the cold
came down. The cold.

I'll keep track of Walter
and hope he'll do the same
for us. But it's over.
It's always good to know

when that is so, and still
when I wake sometimes
I hear our dogs, long gone,
snuffling at dawn.

Running Dog Blues

for Murray

He was in a hurry
like Ornette Coleman
or Pablo Picasso or
Maury Wills, the base thief,
in such a hurry we know
he wants to get there
but also that
      there is no
emergency.
      He was in a hurry.
I wanted to go along
just once to see
what goes by on the way
he went before in such
a hurry the last time
he left us behind.

Dream of Departure

I kept falling into
various bodies of water—
at first a dirty acequia
fed by the Rio Grande,
then a neat rectangle
of chlorine, painted lanes
and pennants flapping overhead.
And last, a stream running clear
over stones and cold enough
for trout.
     I kept getting out
with help from people passing by.
My money was always safe,
dry. And my papers.
         One Samaritan
gave me a key to this room
I had to vacate by noon,
and another, matching fedoras
in grey and black. I didn't know
which to wear, my clothes
soaked and off-color.
         I *did* know
I had to leave the country.
It was urgent.

My passport was dry,
but in my room the tap had dripped
all night, and it was so humid
the packing boxes came apart
in strips and ridges. Useless.
The fedoras lost their shape.
I wasn't about to leave
in such disarray, so I bolted
the door and waited.

Departing LAX

You must avoid
the transportation
at all times
of dangerous items
and keep your bags
under close control.

Those not so in control
will be confiscated. Avoid
handling the bags
of others. Transporting
pointed or explosive items
is at any time

a crime, in this time
especially. Officers at control
points may confiscate items
they fancy, that shine, that fill a void
or promise transport
of a certain kind (bags

of cosmetics or bags
of nylons from your mother's time
may evoke such transport).
Going to and fro, keep control
of your nostalgia, avoiding
woes and kit bags, items

repacking time. Item:
for every day take a bag
to leave behind. Avoid
old friends at exits. Untimely
exchanges soften self-control.
Your transport

will soon be over and the transport
of others, too, whose items
are not yours to control.
Meet no one at the baggage
carousels at any time.
If asked, always avoid

saying how the transportation of bags
may distract one, one item at a time,
until you can't control what to avoid.

Anticipating Retirement, I Explore Guatemala

I.

Trying to save time in Antigua City
I went by the book, from one façade
to the next—café, courtyard, church—
Colonial Spain in grandeur and ruined
by volcano and quake, her clobbered
offices of res publica revived as shops
of jade and Panamas and banks protected
by booted men—no, just boys, in fact,
with zitty complexions and Uzis
standing in the cool scrim of air
between displays and the rising dust
of all those stones fallen down. I try
to keep my saints straight, my Spanish,
simple. "I'd like *papaya licuados. Por favor.*"

2.

Quiero una papaya licuados, por favor.
Mas palabras. Between "bill" and "cost,"
the difference of a consonant. Between
"face" and "dear," a vowel. That's "too dear,"
I practice, then say my numbers. I'd like
to pay in dollars, but I have *quetzales*,
local notes as fanciful as this economy
and, it turns out, too greasy for the Minister
of How Things Look. He has recalled them
without informing the Minister for Making
More. And so: this morning's panic on the square.
The long arcades fill with strapless girls
from Eau Claire, checks in hand, confused
students for change at the going rate.

3.

Students for change? I should stop
settling for irony, starting now. I cross
the square, Greene's exemplary *Power
and Glory* in hand, a straightly told story
of a priest lifted up and hunted down
just north of here. And so: the sun shines
directly. Here comes a man with a Polaroid
hung around his neck who proposes one shot
for three dollars. In advance. I imagine
this prop left or stolen decades ago
and wonder what daily magic of repair
is required, if it works at all. No matter
now that I have paid. The show begins:
he stands me in front of the fountain.

4.

He stands me in front of the fountain
of maidens and tilts my Panama, leaves
me squinting in the sun. It's a good time
to run for it. But no. He gestures left,
then right, then frowns. He has some style,
lifting a finger for stillness. Presto!
Something clicks in the box. He pulls a sheet
and counts out loud. I follow to twenty.
For the finale he rips the exposure free
and waves it above his head as a voyager
might his hanky from the deck. Good-bye!
No. He hands it over and here I am: too heavy,
burned but smiling, spray from eight nipples
of stone behind me: dazed man with nimbus.

5.

Dazed, a nimbus of bugs in sun and shade,
I tour the coffee fields at Jocotenango,
following a well-toned Aussie down the path.
So, too, a woman from Boston, whose husband
has just said we are all obliged to visit Tikal.
He has tickets for tomorrow. I try to keep pace
with the long-legged Aussie, the hairs
on his swollen calves lit like filaments.
So notes the woman from Boston, whose husband
must be more than she can bear in this heat.
We wind through the plants to a wide space
where we find hubcaps filled with the ashes
from the pickers' lunch. Here a bent woman
poses for the husband with her sack.

6.

As the husband posed with her sack,
she clucked, *"Muy verde, muy verde."*
Her beans were not the color we see now
in the plantation shop's diorama, "Plant
to Table." It takes six pounds of "cherry"
beans to make ten of dried that make
twenty-four cups to drink. That means the old woman
(she was eighty, if a day) who this morning picked
about sixty pounds hauled in enough for ten
of these fragrant packages, one of which
I buy for seven dollars, or forty-nine *quetzales*. In the courtyard
several men spread with rakes and slatted skids
the beans pushed into hills and flat again.
Stragglers crack like roaches under their feet.

7.

In the *baños* down the hall, roaches scatter
in light. My first three nights at the *posada*
a mosquito worried my sleep. I couldn't find
her in the morning. My first three nights
the couple across the hall woke everyone
in the early hours: quivers and quavers
and something like a yodel, trills, tremolos—
octaves of corybantic ruckus! What words
we have for love, its making, thrall and thrill.
Some double for other appetites: spent, overspent,
demand, largesse. On the fourth morning
I passed that man on the stairs, and I must say
he didn't *seem* all of that—small, glancing,
his *buenos días* swallowed like mine.

8.

No *"buenos días"* this morning, no greeting
the boys who patrol the square in twos,
in boots and khakis and reflecting shades.
No one looks them in the eye anyway.
But look how fragile! On their thin shoulders
where leather slings bear the weight of Uzis
their blouses fold inward like origami wings.
Their boots shine; their magazines glisten
with packing oil not yet wiped off.
It's possible these boys will grow into their jobs,
learn to swagger like cops in Chicago.
For all I know the Minister for More
Bullets has recalled the rounds, lightening the load
before something awful happens.

9.

Everyone knows something awful happened
at Tikal—whether decades of drought
or disease or the ordinary violence we know.
There must be lessons for us, how such an exact
place so finely engineered can end
without a proper arc. The Long Count stopped
one day. That's all for now. No doubt
they'll start digging and sifting again,
unearthing utensils, listing what's in store,
fitting shards like a jigsaw,
their tables of assorted pieces of an edge
they imagine. The next surface *will* be scratched.
But for the record, I'm afraid that permanence is
a thing of the past, that we have no time to waste.

Last Hours in Antigua City

On the last day I broke the rules: tacos
from the street, near the colonial fountain
(page 52 in the guide) where women pound
and rinse their clothes as always. At noon

they lined up at the grill and I followed:
sizzled meat, cilantro, handfuls of salsa.
We all sat on the parapet to eat.
Later, near dawn: nightmares, stink and sweat.

I slipped up and down the hallway
to the *baños* (the bugs there the color but larger
than coffee beans). At 5:00 a.m. Eduardo
fetched me for the airport in his Fairlane:

no door handle on my side, busted shocks,
a drunk American lollygagging in back.
The cobbled streets rattled us through town,
and the open road was making waves when

Eduardo looked over, asking, *"Enfermo,
señor?"*
    Oh, *sí.*
      "Puerta. Puerta."
        But see! There's no . . .
When I used the window the drunk roused himself.
"Oh, man," he said, "next time take some Cipro.

"One a day. Keep the Aztecs away."
        Mayans,
I said. Mayans. Aztecs were somewhere else.
"Whatever, bro. I'm down." Closing my eyes,
I conjured calm water, a deep cistern.

Window Shopping in a Fever

I dreamed we were shopping
in the colonnade the hour before dawn.
You walked arm in arm with two men
I'd never met, all of you speaking Spanish
so quickly I couldn't follow.
I had no idea you had such command.
When I fell behind and called out,
"Wait, wait up," you kept going.
I stopped to look in a window.

I stood beside a man, a giant
whose top hat grazed the *latillas*.
He was glossy black, in evening dress,
cigar in his teeth, a fifth of Old Crow
in hand. It's Maximón, the Mayan god
of cuckoldry, his limbs restored!
He was admiring a hat tree of fedoras.
He looked me over and said,
"We are both giants . . . in different ways."

I smiled, studied a cabinet
of folding knives and multipurpose tools.
When the three of you walked by the other way,
he followed with his eyes, then turned
and nodded at a sign on the door—
Hours: 9 a.m. to Life. Others
by Appointment. "I like a shopkeeper
who knows his clientele," he said.
"Take care, amigo. Take heed."

Reviewing the Troops in the Ruins

Usually no one famous shows up
in my dreams, but this time President Bush
appears, his blue eyes surprising.
We are walking through a stone arch
into a rally where he is
unwelcome. Ugly murmurs.
"They don't get it," he turns to me,
"all the hard work we do."

To cheer him up I tell a joke
about my dog dragging in
parts of a bird and then puking
the rest on the kitchen tile.
"I will gladly identify
this species," I tell him
I told my wife, "if you will collect
the bones and feathers."

He laughs in appreciation,
his estimate of me risen.
He asks me to sit next to him
on the reviewing stand, next
to the woman with knees sharp
as the corners of boxes. She wears
the dark suit Audrey Hepburn wore
as Holly Golightly. She sneers.

Some soldiers and some time
and some weapons go by.
It's not getting any easier.
Boos and catcalls. A shuffle.
A ruckus in the bleachers.
The point is: I like him,
his eyes not at all what
I imagined. It's time to leave

and quickly, his agents say, it's no good
being out in the open like this.
And we are. I look around and see
we are under the stars at Tikal,
steps crumbling into the hillside.
When I look back, the president is gone
with all the rest. The crowd mutters,
blood thrumming in the ear
of this theater in ruins.

Part IV

Note to Self

Get a grip. It's time
to admit no one's in charge
of working it out
in the end, no ending
of tricks, no explication
of prior contradictions
not *seeming* at all.

You went to all
the fragrant weddings
and all the funerals
you wanted, one of each
for the fool whose socks
finally matched.
No shoes.

And the reviews . . .
My lord! Not even a nod
to past performance,
no handout, no clapping
ingénue, addled,
flattering and floating
out of her gown.

Maybe it's a note
on the Internet but nothing
in print. No question
of standing O's.
The only gasp
you'll get is your own
above the abyss.

So buck up. So be it.
No doctor. No script.

Finishing Touch

It's my idea that god started working
in large format because it was easy
to see mistakes and make adjustments.
No point busting your knuckles or running
to True Value for smaller Dremel tools,
and no getting on your knees to look for
something under the sofa.
        Seriously
it's my idea that once the first blush
wore off and space was needed
for the next project, the pendulum swung
back in an awful hurry. Sure, there's waste
involved in size—large reptiles, for instance,
and the iceberg's tip—but there were kinks
still to work out. That's when every little thing
got twitchy. Tick tock. Tick tock.
        We lost
room for ample mistakes. I'm no chemist,
but I believe we could use more serotonin
on a regular basis. No point skimping!
In this way, I believe, we might escape
the foolish exactitude some of us live by,
how fine we must be, how small.

Fishing the St. Joe

1.

Everything moves at once
around him balancing
at last in the flat water
behind the rock
roughly dividing the water.
The wind clatters
in the asparagus grass
and the late sunlight
skitters upstream on rocks.
Exactly six mallards break
from the grass banking north
in a vee their odd bodies
in flight like bowling pins
knocked sideways sliding
over the braided water
where the cutthroat
hold on the bias
waiting for leftovers.
He sidesteps that way
braced against the current
false casting first for line
then drifting a spent caddis
to water under the willow.
Everything still moves.

2.

Everything   at once
around him balancing
   in the flat water
   the rock
      dividing the water.
The   clatter
   the asparagus grass
   the late sunlight
skitters upstream
      six mallards break
from the   bank north
in a vee   odd bodies
      like bowling pins
knocked sideways
over   braided water
where   cutthroat
   on the bias
wait   for leftovers.
   Sidestep that way
brace against the current
   casting   line
   drifting a   caddis
to   the willow
everything   moves.

3.

Everything
      balancing
         flat water
      the rock
         the water
      clatter
   the   grass
      late sunlight
skitters
      six mallards break
            north
   a vee
      like bowling pins
      sideways
over   water
      cutthroat
hold
      for leftovers
         that way
      against the current
            line
      a spent caddis
      under the willow
         moves.

The Hour for Walking Dogs

And so at the hour for cocktails
and the walking of dogs
my Lab—named Moby for color
and Coyote for his origin
on this high desert—and I
take our seats on the patio
to satisfy our curiosities.
He has three ways to watch
because the house behind us
is old news. I look
straight ahead, thinking back.

Our block's a favorite for walking dogs,
a bit of shade, a school at one end
and church grounds at the other make
a fertile space barely patrolled
by the prudish. Our walkers keep
their plastic bags folded
in obvious pockets and chat on cells
into the air. Such passion wasted!
I have my gin and the dog his bone.
My eye is sharp, his nose keen
for what's in the wind.

A creature of habit, he knows
the score: there's a certain time
for this place, and he's not going
to miss it. I could use his sense
of moment. For me
it's that time of evening
when exercise involves the old days
and friends, or those I thought so,

our informations filed and lost.
The dog and I settle in, but right now
there's not much for us to track

except the early arrivals
for the Tuesday AA that meets
in the church basement. A few
pause and greet on the sidewalk
before going down to folding chairs,
ashtrays, the coffee urn. Moby wets
his nose and collects the sober details
of the day. As usual I think of
calling someone with the news.
In the time we have been here
something has changed for good.

Afterword

You know how the day
gets away from you: it's noon
before you know it and then
cocktails in a blink.

You can't get a word in
edgewise before bed,
and the fitful dark
happens until it's bright

again, too bright for breakfast
on any day, any April
when the rude interruptions—
those yellow tulips

in your neighbor's garden—
flash in the corner
of your eye like a migraine
starting, and you need the dark

again and quiet. It's winter
before you have more coffee.
Across the snowy expanse
of your backyard, smooth

as vellum, a squirrel
makes tracks, an ellipsis
from cherry to fence and beyond
slowly filling in.

Acknowledgments

These poems, sometimes in different versions, have previously appeared in the following journals:

Adobe Walls: "Early Snow," "An Elegy ahead of Time," and "Running Dog Blues"

bosque (the magazine) 3: "The Disambiguation of Katydids" and "Lunch at the Diner"

bosque (the magazine) 4: "The Hour for Walking Dogs," "Making Peace," and "Finishing Touch"

Diagram: "Current Events," "Railing against People Railing against Kansas," "Fishing the St. Joe," and "Revisiting the Weather"

Elysian Fields: "Shagging Flies"

Flint Hills Review: "The State Bird"

Imagination and Place: Weather: "Lucretius Applied on the Great Plains" and "Cleaning Up in October"

Massachusetts Review: "Early Work"

Natural Bridge: Section 1 of "The Salesman"

Night Bomb Review: "Departing LAX" and "Spring Fever Blues"

Prairie Schooner: "Reviewing the Troops in the Ruins"

Santa Fe Review: "Fall Leaves Blues" and "Window Shopping in a Fever"

In addition, many of these poems appeared in *Walter's Yard* (2013) and *The Disambiguation of Katydids* (2015), both chapbooks printed by Kattywompus.